Modern Calligraphy

20 DIY Calligraphy Projects For Creating Beautiful Lettered Art

Table of content

Introduction 3
Chapter 1 – Card Art..5
Chapter 2 – Using Letters for Pictures...10
Chapter 3 – Making a Picture of Words 14
Chapter 4 – Quotes and Poems 19
Chapter 5 – Variations and Other Tips and Tricks...24
Conclusion 29

Introduction

You are looking for a new hobby, but everything seems so common and mainstream. So what are you going to do that is different, fun, and yet creative all at the same time?

There are all kinds of fiber arts out there, and then there is baking and cooking. You can do woodworking, or you could embrace an entirely new craft. So how are you going to choose?

Go with something new and fresh, and what is cooler than calligraphy? It is a dual purpose kind of art, and you can start doing it right now, even if you don't know how to do calligraphy. You don't need to have any prior calligraphy experience to be able to do calligraphy art, and you are going to discover a world that is fresh and new.

But I don't have any idea what I am doing... you tell yourself. But that's ok. You can do this today with nothing more than a calligraphy pen and a piece of paper. If you want to get more elaborate, all you have to do is change the kind of pen or paper you are using, and you are set.

There isn't an art form that is both easy and as fun as this, because there are so many different directions you can go in with just your pen and paper. There is so much more to calligraphy art than just words, and you are going to learn how to express yourself in a whole new way.

Can you imagine being able to put your emotions into a picture, with more than just words? They say that a picture is worth a thousand words, but you are going to be able to paint a picture with your words.

It is so much more beautiful than anything that you have ever seen before, and you are going to have all of your gift problems solved. Imagine being able to say just what you want to say with your gift. No more searching for the right card, no more hoping for the right quote.

With calligraphy art, you are free to express yourself in ways that you have only dreamed of before. This is a whole new way of doing things, and you are going to fall in love with the freedom that is yours to take.

So what are you waiting for? There is a whole new world out there that is just waiting for you to jump in and make your mark for good.

Paint a world of words.

Chapter 1 – Card Art

No matter what the occasion is, there is always a reason to give a card. When you are giving a card, you want to make it the best that it can be. There are times when you only need to give a card to say exactly what you want to say, and bring a smile to your friend's face.

On the other hand, you might be getting ready to have a big event in your life, and you want to have the best cards available for that event. When you are making these cards, you are able to do exactly what you want with each and every card.

So go ahead and express yourself. You can't do it wrong, and you are going to love how personal you can make these!

Birthday cards

What you will need:

Card paper

Ink

Pen

Glitter

Directions:

Use a steady hand, and dip your pen in ink. When you are making a birthday card, you want to make it elaborate and beautiful. Use plenty of swoops with the letters and make it say exactly what you want it to say.

You can use glitter ink, or you can always add the glitter while the ink is still wet. The important thing to note is that you don't want it to bleed, so only use paper that holds the ink well.

Let dry and your card is ready!

Special invitations

What you will need:

Card paper

Ink

Pen

Plastic card cover

Directions:

For invitations, you want to say something on the front that announces that the recipient is invited to some event. You can do this with a simple "you're invited" or something that is along those lines.

Let dry, then on the inside, write the details of the event. You will want to do this in a less elaborate hand, and make the directions clear. Some people opt to do this in regular print and keep the calligraphy for the outer portion of the card, but that is up to you.

Let it all dry, and add any extra features that you wanted to have on the card. When it is dry, you can slip it in a card cover... these can be purchased at any craft store, and you are ready to send out your card!

Make sure that you use paper that doesn't bleed the ink, and let it all dry completely before moving on with the next steps. These can take a while to make, but you are going to be happier with the results.

Announcements

What you will need:

Ink

Pen

Card paper

Card covers

Extra décor

Directions:

For your announcement, you are going to need to place the extra décor first. Do this by placing it in a place where you won't hit it where you are writing, but also to where you know there is enough room for you to write.

When the glue is dry, use your pen and ink to write the main announcement on the front of the card in an elaborate font. Make the announcement short and to the point, then fill in the details inside the card.

Let everything dry completely between steps, and when it is all dry, slide it into a card cover before you put it in an envelope.

Use paper that won't bleed, and glue that dries clear. As a rule of thumb, less is more with the glue and the ink.

Cards for all occasions

What you will need:

Card paper

Glue

Ink

Pen

Glitter

Décor

Card cover

Directions:

No matter what the occasion is, you are going to need the same basic components to make the card. Always start with the extra piece, then do the ink on the front of the card.

Next do the filler ink inside the card, then finish with the glitter if you are going to use it. Make sure it is all dry before you move on, and as a finishing touch slide the card into the card cover.

Always use paper that is going to hold the ink and the extra things you choose to put on your card, and use space. You don't ever want to crowd the letters on any card, as the art is going to be ruined in the appearance of crowding.

You are going to get the hang of it as you practice, so don't get discouraged if it doesn't go well at first.

Chapter 2 – Using Letters for Pictures

It is a common choice for a tattoo to use a foreign word as the making of the piece, but did you know that you can do this for yourself in calligraphy? You can make a beautiful picture with nothing more than a letter or two, and you can embellish all kinds of pictures with the same idea.

These are all pieces that you can make with just letters, and you can express yourself in such awe inspiring ways even you are going to be impressed. Take your time and work each letter as best as you can. There is no rush, and art is always better if you are pouring your soul in with your work.

Inspirational pictures

What you will need:

Poster board

Ink

Large pen

Poster picture

Directions:

If you can, use transfer paper to take the picture and put it on the poster board. If this isn't possible, then use the picture as an accent to what you are doing, and glue it to the corner of the board.

You are going to want to use poster board as this tends to hold the ink better. When you are ready, use your pen and ink to put whatever letter you feel is best to pair with the picture. This can be an entire word, one letter, or use the same letter multiple times as a boarder.

Express yourself and see what happens.

Using letters as art

What you will need:

Neutral colored poster board

Ink

Pen

Directions:

It is time to get fancy with this one. Use your pen and dip it in the ink, you are going to be generous with the ink on this one, and make an elaborate letter. You can do individual letters, or you can make initials.

Any way you want to express yourself with the minimal amount of letters is the way to go with this project, just make sure that it is completely dry before you cover it with a frame or plastic cover.

Experiment with different kinds of ink and pens, and see what you can come up with. There are times when this is the most powerful art form you can imagine. So go for it!

Painting on the pictures

What you will need:

Poster board

Paint

Paint brush

Ink

Pen

Directions:

Start by using your paint brush and paint, and make a large letter on the poster board. It can be any letter that you want, just make sure that you make it big and elaborate. Lots of swirls.

Let dry.

Next, use your ink and pen, and make a second letter inside the first letter, you can either copy the same letter and make it a smaller version inside of the bigger one, or you can again go with initials and make them slightly overlap.

The point is that you are using the paint to make a large and impressive letter, then using the ink to make a smaller and more deliberate letter inside of the first one. The second letter is going to be more defined, and the bigger one is going to be flashier.

You can also use the ink to outline the larger letter and pull the picture together better. No matter how you do it, you are going to want to use the two separate components and pull them together as one. Think of harmony and working together on this one to pull the entire work together.

Sometimes a back drop is going to help you along with this, but that is up to you. express yourself.

Using letters on letters

What you will need:

Poster board

Ink

Pen

Paint

Paintbrush

Directions:

Start with the poster board, and a large paintbrush. Make a large letter with the paint, then slightly overlap with a second letter in the paint. If you want, you can use two different colors of paint to add depth and intrigue.

Let dry completely, then bring in your ink and pen. Use the pen to make elaborate swirls and swoops on the paint. You don't need to make a full word, and you don't need to worry about making sense so to speak.

The point of calligraphy art is to make beauty out of the letters themselves, and sometimes the best way to do that is to pair letters that look good together simply because they do. You can focus on the same basic shape, the same letter in different fonts, or the same letter in different sizes.

Play around with it and see what it is you like, and work with it until you are happy with it. If you are using poster board, you aren't going to have to worry about it bleeding, and always make sure you let each letter dry before you proceed to the next.

The one thing that is going to make this difficult is not waiting for the letters to dry, and smearing them as you work.

Patience is key, and when you are using it, you are going to be amazed at the beauty that is found in just a single letter.

Chapter 3 – Making a Picture of Words

They say that a picture is worth a thousand words, and you can do so much with turning words into pictures. Again with the tattoo idea, you can say so much with a single word that an entire sentence can't even convey.

Pick a picture that is full of color and life, and label it with the word that comes to mind the most. Don't stress about this, and never try too hard. Simply look at it and think about what you feel when you see it, and what word comes to mind. When you are doing this enough, you are going to see pictures in a whole new light, and you are going to start feeling what you are seeing.

Words are going to become art, and your pictures are going to invoke feelings in your viewers that the sight alone never could. Take your time and practice, and see what you can come up with.

Inspiring words

What you will need:

Poster board

Pen

Ink

Picture

Glue

Directions:

The idea behind this is to use a word to stir up an emotion with the picture that you have chosen. I want you to choose the word first, then use your pen and ink to make it elaborate on the board.

Next, I want you to find the picture that best conveys this word in the way that you want it to be conveyed. When you do this, you are going to see that the word takes on a whole new meaning.

It is a way to close down the interpretation of your art, and make it more straightforward.

Glue the picture onto the board, and let it all dry.

Using words to sum up a picture

What you will need:

Poster board

Picture

Glue

Ink

Pen

Directions:

In a way, this is a project that is worked backwards from the last project. I want you to find a picture that you love, and print it out then glue it to the poster board. Again, it is very important that you leave enough room on the poster board for the ink to sit on the board directly, you don't want it to bleed.

When your picture is glued on and the glue is dry, use your ink and your pen to write the word that you feel is best for the picture. Do what you want to do here, don't think, feel. The more you are able to dig deep and express from your emotions, the better your art is going to turn out.

Let it dry, and your art is ready for display.

Fancy script

What you will need:

Poster board

Ink

Glitter ink

Pen

Directions:

This is a very simply, yet effective art project. I want you to take the poster board and the ink, and simply write a word in the most beautiful handwriting you have. This is going to take some practice to get just what you want, but with time you are going to be able to make a word that is a work of art in and of itself.

When the first word is dry, you can take the second ink and either outline the first word that you have written, or write it again slightly off to the side so you have almost a repeated effect.

Take your time and mess around with it, see what you come up with and what you like. As I have said before, there is no wrong way to do this, and the more you are able to express yourself, the easier it is going to be to express yourself.

A picture worth a thousand words

What you will need:

Paint

Poster board

Ink

Paint brush

Pen

Directions:

For this project, I want you to start by picking the word that you are going to use, then use your paint and paintbrush to paint the word on your poster board in a different language.

It isn't hard to find the word in a different language thanks to the internet these days, and you can make a vastly different piece using the same word but different languages. When you are finished with the initial painting, it is time to add in the calligraphy.

Towards the bottom right hand portion of the picture, I want you to write that same word in English in the calligraphy style of your choice. Be elaborate and be showy, and you are going to be amazed at the beauty that comes forth from such a simple idea.

Make sure that everything is dry before you move on to the next steps in the project, and make sure it is all dry before you hang it up for display. Try using the same word, in three different base languages, then hang them all up side by side in your living room to display.

Chapter 4 – Quotes and Poems

When you pull together art and poetry, it is like you are combining magic and miracles. There is so much to be said in art, and there is so much that is said in poetry. It is an epic way you can combine what has been said so long ago, with the art that you are now feeling.

If you would like to come up with something that is entirely you, write your own quotes and poetry for these projects. Just because they haven't been said before doesn't mean that they aren't worth you writing, and the more you preserve your words the more people are going to be influenced by them.

Think of the poetry and quotes in terms of how you feel when you hear them, and write to reflect that. Think of it as two artists working together, separated by years and miles, but drawn together with a common purpose. You are going to be amazed by what you are able to produce.

Quotes for a picture

What you will need:

Poster board

Glue

Ink

Pen

Picture

Quote

Directions:

First you need your picture and the quote that you are going to use. You can print out the picture, but you are going to need to use the calligraphy to write and poem.

Make sure you are writing on board that won't bleed, and that it dries before you assemble. When you are ready, place the picture first, and the quote over the pic, but off to the side enough that you can still see what the picture is.

It is a really easy way to make your own inspirational quotes and pics for any room in your home.

Quotes on a picture

What you will need:

Poster board

Glue

Ink

Pen

Plastic covers (can be purchased at any craft store)

Picture

Directions:

This is a little trickier, but you start with gluing the picture to the poster board, then slide the plastic cover over the top. Glue in place. Next, take the section of poster board that you are going to write on, and write the quote in the best calligraphy you have.

Glue this on top of the pic, and slide another cover over the top. Glue this one in place as well. Make sure you are waiting for everything to dry in between steps, and that you are placing it all so you can comfortably see it.

Poems art

What you will need:

Poster board

Poem

Ink

Pen

Directions:

All you really need for this is poster board with plenty of room for your poem, and the time and patience to work on it. Find a poem that you love, and write it out in your best handwriting.

This sounds easy enough at first, but if you aren't going to take your time, you are going to have a disaster. Make sure you are spelling everything correctly, that you are spacing it to where it needs to be to fit on your board, and that you have confident loops in your writing.

Things like this are using your skills directly as the art. Sure you are going to see the beauty of the words as well, but what they are going to see as art is the way that it is written, and that falls directly back on your calligraphy handwriting.

Take your time and make the most of the opportunity, and you are going to have all kinds of requests for other poems and quotes.

Poems for pics

What you will need:

Poster board

Poem

Ink

Picture

Pen

Glue

Directions:

Start with either the poem or the pic, and find the other that matches what the poem or pic makes you think of. This is the same idea as the quote and the poem for art combined.

Use your best handwriting, take the time to make sure that it is all dry, and place items on your board so everyone can see what you are trying to say. You never want to crowd or squish these things together, and you don't want to make it look rushed.

Take your time and see the beauty in the project as a whole, and your consideration is going to shine through in your finished work of art.

Chapter 5 – Variations and Other Tips and Tricks

All too often those that are in calligraphy tend to limit themselves to the standard of pen and paper. This is all too limiting and it isn't what this kind of art is about. You need to take your skills to the next level with all kinds of different ways you can express your talent.

Use your imagination and think of new ways you can show the world what you can do with words and writing, and you may even surprise yourself with some of the things you can think of.

This is a whole new world that is opened up to you, so make the most of it and make it say what you want it to say.

You won't regret anything that you try.

Inks galore

What you will need:

Calligraphy paper

Inks

Pen

Ink cleaner

Pen pad

Directions:

I want you to let your imagination run wild with this one. Use the ink that comes to mind and write what you are moved to write. It doesn't need to make sense per se, and you don't have to worry that anyone is going to understand what you are saying.

I don't want you to start fresh when you use new ink, and I don't want you to think that you can mess this up. Just give your ink time to dry in between the time that you change to a new ink, and start again.

Use big words, big letters, elaborate letters and words, and the small and simple. Use it all in one piece of paper, and see the image come to life right before your eyes.

That is what art is about, doing what you think feels right at the time, and letting it all come together as it does.

Paint and canvas

What you will need:

Canvas

Paint

Paint brushes in various sizes

Directions:

For this project I want you to follow any of the other directions for the previous art projects that I have mentioned, but I want you to take your skills to the canvas with paint and paint brushes.

No ink or pens to be found, just use the paint and brushes, and say what you need to say. There is a lot of freedom that comes from using paint and brushes, as you can make so many different shapes that can be hard to accomplish with a pen.

Have fun with it and see what comes out of your imagination, use different sizes of brushes and different kinds of paint, all in one. You are going to love what you come up with, and you may even be surprised at what you are able to do with just paint and canvas.

It is like opening up an entire new realm with just the changing of the two modems you are using.

Let your imagination run wild.

Variation station

What you will need:

Ink

Paper

Canvas

Paint

Paint brushes

Directions:

Take the two previous projects, and combine them into one with this project here. I want you to get creative, to say what you want, and to use what you want to do it. Combine the ink and the paint, and the pens and the brushes.

The world is at your fingertips and all you need to do is let your creativity go and see what you are able to come up with. There is so much that you can do with the combination of the two of these, you may be surprised at how much creativity is bubbling up inside of you, just waiting to get out.

All you need to remember is that you have to let it all dry before you change to a new color or ink, and you are going to be just fine.

Wood art

What you will need:

Wood burner

Pencil

Wood

Directions:

For this last project, I want to take a step away from ink and paint, and I want you to be able to make a more permanent feature. Use wood, and a pencil to sketch on the wood what you want to say, then use a wood burner to carefully burn into the wood exactly what you wrote with the pencil.

This is going to take a little more time than with ink and pen, but you are going to be saved the dry time. It is a slower method in some ways, a faster method in others, but I guarantee you are going to fall in love with the results.

I hope you enjoyed the projects that I have provided in this book, and I highly encourage you to explore your creativity. You can't do this wrong, and you are going to love what you are able to make with just pen and paper. Or anything else that you decide to use is going to be amazing, too!

Get ready to wow your friends and family, and to embrace a new art that has been around as long as time itself.

Happy writing.

Conclusion

There you have it, a whole new way to express yourself through your art. You are going to find that this is the most addicting kind of art that there is. You can say what you need to say, you can make beauty with the words, and you can make things to give to your friends and family.

Feel free to use variations and any other way of expressing yourself. You don't have to stick with just the pen and paper way of doing things, as you saw in the last section of art, there are all kinds of ways you can use thus kind of art to express yourself.

If you are happy with the results, and if you are able to say what you want with your art, then you are doing it right. I don't want you to hold yourself back with the fear that you may do it wrong, and I don't want you to think that other people are going to judge you for your art.

There is no way you can express yourself wrong, and when you are following the calligraphy as a guide, you are going to see that there are countless ways you can take these suggestions and make them your own. I want you to have fun with this, and I want you to be able to have fun with this.

Calligraphy is an art and a form of communication, and it is something that has been around for centuries. People of all ages and in all different cultures have been able to show the world what they want to say with their words, and now you can, too.

Embrace the artist that is in you, and unleash the scribe that is just begging to be let out. You can do it, and you can do it well. As long as you are having fun while you do it, and if you are happy with what you are producing, you are doing it right.

Get yourself different kinds of paper, then move on to other platforms, and start with ink at first, but move on to other ways of writing as well. Experiment until you find what you like the best, and practice until you are able to do it as you would like.

Art is expression, and you have it inside of you. Every time you feel an emotion, and every time you see something and feel that inspiration, you have art inside that is just asking to be let out. Now is the time to let that out, and calligraphy is the way to do it.

So what are you waiting for? Let it out and let it go.

www.ingramcontent.com/pod-product-compliance
Lightning Source LLC
Chambersburg PA
CBHW050036230526
45470CB00003B/1314

Copyright © by Lon S. Safko

All rights reserved. No part of this book may be used or reproduced by any means, graphic, electronic, or mechanical, including photocopying, recording, taping or by any information storage retrieval system without the written permission of the publisher except in the case of brief quotations embodied in critical articles and reviews.

Printed in the United States of America

This book was created using 100% recycled electrons

No animals were harmed in the making of this book

This book is dolphin safe

Never Give Up!
An Entrepreneur's Success Guide
Top 10 Lessons Learned

During the 30 years of my career, I've built 14 companies. Some were mushroom cloud failures, while others were very successful. Throughout this process, some of my decisions led to success and others led to the mushroom clouds. I analyzed and questioned those decisions to determine what would have taken me down a different path. Here's an example of each company case scenario: